SandCastle

Word Families Set 8

-ake as in cake

Carey Molter

Consulting Editor Monica Marx, M.A./Reading Specialist

Published by SandCastle™, an imprint of ABDO Publishing Company, 4940 Viking Drive, Edina, Minnesota 55435.

Printed in the United States.

Credits
Edited by: Pam Price
Curriculum Coordinator: Nancy Tuminelly
Cover and Interior Design and Production: Mighty Media
Photo Credits: BananaStock Ltd., Hemera, PhotoDisc

Library of Congress Cataloging-in-Publication Data

Molter, Carey, 1973-
    -Ake as in cake / Carey Molter.
       p. cm. -- (Word families. Set VIII)
    Summary: Introduces, in brief text and illustrations, the use of the letter combination "ake" in such words as "cake," "snake," "brake," and "lake."
    ISBN 1-59197-270-1
    1. Readers (Primary) [1. Vocabulary. 2. Reading.] I. Title.

PE1119 .M583 2003
428.1--dc21
                                          2002038211

SandCastle™ books are created by a professional team of educators, reading specialists, and content developers around five essential components that include phonemic awareness, phonics, vocabulary, text comprehension, and fluency. All books are written, reviewed, and leveled for guided reading, early intervention reading, and Accelerated Reader® programs and designed for use in shared, guided, and independent reading and writing activities to support a balanced approach to literacy instruction.

Let Us Know

After reading the book, SandCastle would like you to tell us your stories about reading. What is your favorite page? Was there something hard that you needed help with? Share the ups and downs of learning to read. We want to hear from you! To get posted on the ABDO Publishing Company Web site, send us e-mail at:

sandcastle@abdopub.com

SandCastle Level: Beginning

-ake Words

cake

drake

lake

rake

snake

stake

The cake has 24 candles on it.

A drake is a male duck.

There are boats on the lake.

Mrs. Blake picks up
leaves with a rake.

The snake is black and yellow.

Billy uses a stake to
hold down the tent.

Jake the Drake

This is Jake.

Jake is a drake.

He lives by the lake.

Jake likes to bake.

Jake makes a cake.

The snake
smells the cake.

The snake
goes up the rake.

Jake sees his mistake!

Jake gives the rake
a shake.

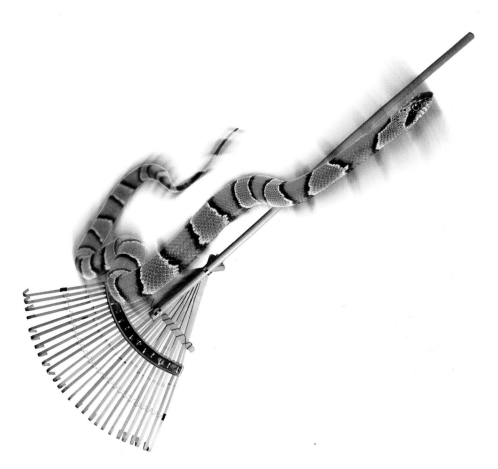

The snake
begins to quake.

The snake and the rake
go in the lake.

No more cake
for that snake!

The -ake Word Family

bake	mistake
brake	Mrs. Blake
cake	quake
drake	rake
fake	shake
Jake	snake
lake	stake
make	take

Glossary

Some of the words in this list may have more than one meaning. The meaning listed here reflects the way the word is used in the book.

cake   a baked dessert made with flour, eggs, sugar, and butter

drake   a male duck

lake   a body of fresh water surrounded by land

rake   a garden tool used for gathering leaves

stake   a peg with a hook on the end used to hold down a tent

About SandCastle™

A professional team of educators, reading specialists, and content developers created the SandCastle™ series to support young readers as they develop reading skills and strategies and increase their general knowledge. The SandCastle™ series has four levels that correspond to early literacy development in young children. The levels are provided to help teachers and parents select the appropriate books for young readers.

Emerging Readers
(no flags)

Beginning Readers
(1 flag)

Transitional Readers
(2 flags)

Fluent Readers
(3 flags)

These levels are meant only as a guide. All levels are subject to change.

To see a complete list of SandCastle™ books and other nonfiction titles from ABDO Publishing Company, visit **www.abdopub.com** or contact us at:

4940 Viking Drive, Edina, Minnesota 55435 • 1-800-800-1312 • fax: 1-952-831-1632